MW01716782

To order additional copies of **Stereo Memories**, for each copy desired send $10.00 check, cash, or money order to:

Bowman James Publishing House
Attn: Jim Sharp
7 Prospect Court
Brookfield, CT 06804

Stereo Memories

Poetry by Jim Sharp

Jim Sharp

Bowman James Publishing House
Attn: Jim Sharp
7 Prospect Court
Brookfield, CT 06804

ISBN 0-9647155-0-3

Poetry by Jim Sharp

Printed in the United States of America

For Mom and Dad

Table of Contents

Love

Pain

Smiles

Sonnets

Stereo Memories

Love

I Look at You

I look at you, and what do I see?
A pretty young face looking back at me.
You've not aged at all, not even a bit.
So pretty, so young, so delicate.
Oh I know there's a wrinkle under your chin,
but it goes away when you flash a grin.
And so what if there's a gray hair or two.
Silver is precious as so are you.
Maybe your breasts are sagging a tad,
but they're still a turn on for this lad.
Oh I guess your waist is a little thicker,
but then so is mine, so let's not bicker.
I look at you, and what do I see?
A pretty young mother looking back at me.
A son over thirty, that must be a lie.
Why, you can't be more than twenty-five.
Grandchildren too, surely you jest.
With the fountain of youth, you are blessed.
I look at you, and what do I see?
A pretty young wife who is part of me.
To love with and share with until time finally ends,
or maybe forever, we'll still be friends.

I Ought to be Working

I ought to be working, but I'm not.
I'm writing a poem as I do oft.

I may lose my job, sometimes I don't care.
My thoughts drift away to the things that we share.

Our bodies, our minds, and many good times.
My job motivation's not worth a dime.

I'm lost in you as I often am.
Nothing else is worth a damn.

My boss is coming, it won't be good tidings.
But a click of the mouse, and this poem is hiding.

And my real work is there for any to see,
and this poem's a secret between you and me.

Why can't you ever stay out of my mind?
I need to do some work sometimes.

I guess I'll start working to earn a few tens,
but say do you remember when . . . . . .?

Make the Angels Dance

I wish there was something that I could do
They brought me life so long ago
But more important they loved me too
and I couldn't believe that they would go
Time keeps on it just won't pause
They're not the only ones growing old
And I continue to look for a cause
for birth, for life, for being bold
Dad's already gone, I've told him goodbye
The house I loved is empty now
Time has passed the tears are dry
But still I wonder what and how
the reason is for all of this
for man and woman love one flesh
the fleeting times of tender bliss
when hearts and bodies finally mesh
Perhaps that is the reason why
We're born to live but have to die
But in between we have that chance
To try and make the angels dance
So yes there's something I can do
I can live and love and ever be true
To the legacy that they left to me
and to the ones I love and they love me
To be strong and pure and not afraid
Until the new begins and the old will fade.

I'm Not Sure

I'm not really sure
what love is.
Perhaps skin touching skin
warming each other.
eyes meeting still causing
a chill up your back.
still holding hands in church
snuggling at night
falling asleep while touching
each other.
fighting forgiving respecting
being honest but holding back
sometimes.
being alone together
comfortably.
sometimes talking
sometimes silent.
a warm breath on
the back of your neck.
a head lying
on your shoulder.
Perhaps

First Love

I saw a bumpersticker the other day
"A guy never forgets his first love"
Every once in a while
I see a smile
a nose
a walk
I hear a voice
a laugh
a song
I feel a warmth
an ache
a yearning
I shed some tears
feeling
wondering
what she looks like now
where is she
It all comes back
the warmth
the pain
the love
everything
like it was yesterday
A lot of truth
a lot of memories
in that bumpersticker

Visitors

Are they here some say they are?
Did they come from beyond the stars
or deep in the earth where we cannot go?
I wonder if they're friend or foe.
Perhaps they came from a different time
back to visit their ancestral kind.
Are they us in a million years,
and why did they now decide to appear?
Some say we're part of a giant test.
Are we only guinea pigs inside our nest?
We marvel at their wondrous ships.
"UFOs" we call those blips.
So fast and high we can't begin.
We only dream of catching the wind.
Are we only part of some child's game,
watching, laughing while we pass the blame?

Does our life mean more than this,
or are we only a bowl of fish?
Maybe they with their brilliant minds
see something missing from their time.
Could they be here to learn what it cost
when science became God, and love was lost?
Did they return to the dawn of time
to watch and learn about our kind?
Do we have anything left to teach,
or is it too late are we out of reach?
Will our hate and fear turn them away,
or do we still have something to say
about goodness and love that is for them too,
for all God's creatures out in the blue?
Think about it my new and wonderful friends.
Isn't it worth learning to love again?

Tomorrows

The years have flown, I've stopped counting now.
It seems like yesterday that we took our vow.
Does time go on when we're in love like this,
and does it stand still when we share a kiss?

Time doesn't stand still, the kids have grown up.
A short time ago, the dogs were just pups.
And our baby's a mother, can it really be true?
Somehow I'm happy, but also blue.

Do I really want to know what the future holds?
One day at a time, thus says the Lord.
But my faith is so small, I worry so much.
Will I always be out of touch?

Others went on, someday we will follow.
But I'm afraid I'm not ready to go tomorrow.
Or next week, or next year.
Why do I live in this state of fear?

When I cross the bridge, will there still be you?
We've been together forever, so it must be true.
On the other side, what will I see?
Will you be there, still loving me?

Yes, I'm afraid of dying and of being forgotten?
How long before there's no recollection?
What is eternity, is there such a thing,
or is eternal chaos the name of the game?

Did He really go on to prepare a place,
leaving us here in a state of grace?
Did it really happen, or is it a hoax?
a laughing matter, a little joke?

But in the midst of chaos is beauty and love,
How did it get there, if not from above?
throwing us together, you and me,
to be together through eternity.

Passion

When the passion dies, what is left?
Is it holding hands with the TV set?

Is love still alive when the fire dies?
Or is it nothing more than an empty lie?

If the longing is there, but the body's not willing,
Do we just lie there and stare at the ceiling?

Or do we hold each other and sympathize,
and wonder why the passion died?

We

It still seems strange after such a long time,
we still lie together, our bodies intertwined.

Others have separated, drifted apart.
Why are we different? What welded our hearts?

Why do we have ecstasy, but others sorrow?
Will we be so lucky tomorrow?

Ah Love, My Love

Ah Love, my Love,
Let us fly away, and stay together in our hideaway.
Ah Love, my Love,
Are you ready to swoon and let me take you to the moon?
Ah Love, my Love,
With sensuous lips, from your womanhood, can I take a nip?
Ah Love, my Love,
Of the soft flowing hair, such ecstasy we will share.
Ah Love, my Love,
With the angel eyes, what secrets lie behind your eyes?
Ah Love, my Love,
Of the soft fair skin, when are you going to let me in?
Ah Love, my Love,
I can get drunk on you. Isn't that what you want, too?
Ah Love, my Love,
Let me love you tonight,
and do anything to make it right,
with both of us lost in ecstasy,
Love, dear Love, it was meant to be — you and me for eternity.

Ecstasy

What is ecstasy,
I'm not really sure.
Is it screaming with passion
when we have not a care?

Is it holding and touching
and you know it's for real?
You look at each other
trying to sense what you feel.

Is it loving each other
even when you're apart?
And though miles away,
you still touch your hearts.

Is it staying together
sometimes when its tough?
And you talk it out
to smooth out the rough.

Is it warming each other
through a long winter night?
While waiting for springtime,
and trading love bites.

Maybe ecstasy
is all of the above.
just being together,
and sharing your love.

Soulmates

What is a soulmate, is it me and you?
The first time I saw you, I felt it was true.

I'd had pain in my heart for such a long time.
My motivation for life wasn't worth a dime.

We did not speak, but I knew you were there.
Hope came back, the first time in years.

Is there such a thing as love at first sight?
I know there is for I felt it that night.

We've stayed together for many years.
We laughed a lot and shed some tears.

We raised some kids and a lot of pups
and wore out a couple of pickup trucks.

We laugh, we love, and it's still getting better.
Remember that day we knelt at the altar?

I know someday, we'll be past our prime,
and soon after that, we'll be out of time.

But let's hold each other until that day,
and then face it together, come what may.

Seasons

Year after year we hear nature sing
of Summer Fall Winter and Spring
Spring the new leaps into life
knowing trusting learning to breathe
not yet seeing the pain so rife
the faithful trees beginning to leave.
Summer the blooms leap out in joy
painting the land in colorful hues
playgrounds dense with girls and boys
fields of corn as if on cue.
Autumn beneath that harvest moon
color subdued under that ghostly light
but the morning sun sings an artist's tune
and the trees explode in color so bright.
Winter slips in death covers the earth
in a blanket of white so cold and pristine
but underneath awaiting rebirth
those seasons of life sleeping 'til Spring.

Pain

What Are You Going to Do?

Sometimes I wonder what you're going to do
with the rest of your life.
Is it all really that important?
The pace, the constant on the go?
Is exhaustion a requirement for living if
you never see the autumn,
the sunset, the full moon?
if you never feel
snowflakes against your face,
or a warm rain drenching your clothes,
and you laugh about it?
if you never make love as if nothing else mattered?
if you never listen to the music of
your heartbeat, your breathing, the silence?
if you never get lost in time,
just having fun,
just playing, just loving,
putting it off for another time?
Another year?
Another life?
Everything on a schedule,
same time, same place, next week,
next month, next year,
next life?

The Age

Maybe it really is an age you're going through?
I'd like to believe that it's not really me, but
as I think back over the years.
I have to wonder.
What about before we grew old?
Was it always an act?
You sit there doing your sewing,
watching TV.
Watch one channel, tape another.
Talk on the phone.
Attend to grandchildren.
Never go to bed early, energy unlimited.
And I sit there next to you, touching you,
smelling you, making love to you in my mind,
aching for you to make a move for me.
always hoping, but it never happens.
Never.
And I mustn't make the move because
it's not on today's schedule.
So I continue to disintegrate,
And soon it will all be finished.

Will the Roses Be There?

I guess it's an old cliche now.
Take time to stop and smell the roses.
I know you're busy, and you say that
next year will be different.
But the roses will die, and you say that
they'll be back next year.
But wasn't it this year
that was going to be different?
Everything dies.
Everyone dies,
and it's always too soon.
Isn't it time
to lay in the grass
and close your eyes?
To let it tickle your neck,
to smell, to hear, to feel,
to see with your eyes still closed?
Is it really worth it to wait
until next year?
Isn't it time now?
Are you really sure
that the roses will be there forever?
Are you really sure
that the roses will be there next year?

Train Whistles at Night

In memory of Dolores Sharp

A train whistle at night so faint so far
growing closer and louder as it matures
She bloomed for awhile like a fleeting song
whistling and screaming as she passed along
but started to fade into the night
struggling and crying but losing the fight
as all was passed to the young and the brave
on her lonely journey into the grave.
I lie in bed hearing the sounds
crickets, cicadas, train whistles abound
relaxing, soothing easing my pain
Perhaps it's not all in vain
She lived she died in between she tried
to love and play until she said goodbye
to laugh and cry and take a chance
to make a better world during her dance.
Like the train our lives will fly
and soon we'll all have to die
The past has flown, today's our chance
to try and make a difference
in a world gone mad and for her so wrong
so much pain and too little song
for one who deserved more joy in life
and died alone at last free from strife.

Together Apart

It's too late now
we each have our own life
working all the time
doing other things
without each other
We still see each other
talk together
sleep together
separate lives
sharing a house
a blanket to each other
on cold nights
still better than
an electric blanket
and cheaper
but we lost it
the world moved in
defeated us
living together
apart

Busybody

I'm a busybody yes it's true
always something else to do
crafts to make
calls to take
notes to write
into the night
people to see
a busy bee
kids to call
trips to the mall
meetings to run
under the gun
got to go
time's running low
feed the cat
a spouse what's that
he has to wait
though it's late
I guess to him
I'm now a bore
He knows how
to find the door.

Be a Man

Tough thinking about it
gray hair sagging flesh (wrinkles)

Hard getting up in the morning
stiff never rested enough (arthritis)

Trying to make love
not always able (depressed)

Wondering why
how much time is left (tired)

Afraid to go on
afraid not to (alone)

Still a real man
not crying (macho)

Hide it from everyone
a coverup (lonely)

Keep up the act
Be a man (die)

More Important Things to Do

I love you so much believe me it's true
but I've more important things to do.
I know you've helped me dry my tears
and you've always been there for many years.
You've tried your best for such a long long time.
I think the problem is not yours but mine.
Why I would rather watch TV
than make love to you is way beyond me.
Or go shopping or talk with my friends
is something I cannot comprehend.
But I really want to be a good wife
and to help you fulfill your needs in life.
I know for a man it must be rough
but you should put me first even if its tough.
I've more important things to do
and I feel guilty if you lie there and stew.
Don't make me feel guilty like that
just because that's not where I'm at.
I need my energy for more important things.
If you must make your own chimes ring.

I have things to mend and meetings to attend.
To everything else my time I'll lend.
I'll play with the kids til I'm totally worn
and have nothing left to toot your horn.
But don't you dare go out on me
because that is wrong I'm sure you agree.
And I'm your wife until the end
but it's not my way to bend.
You've got to accept me hangups and all
so take a cold shower or go to the mall.
And tomorrow night won't be good
so don't expect me to be in the mood.
The night after that don't even try
and don't give me that look in your eye.
That's the way I am and will always be.
We just don't share the same cup of tea.
I'm sorry if you lie awake at night
but I need my sleep or I won't feel right.
But we'll talk about it when the lights are low
during the commercials of the TV shows.
I love you so much believe me it's true
but I've more important things to do.

Why Did They Come?

Why did they come?
For some reason it was meant
for them to rule this land
to rule us.

Why did they kill the buffalo
rape our women
kill our children
kill us?

They professed freedom for all.
But it was only words.
They came they killed.
It was only words.

We took the buffalo
for food for clothing for life.
They took the buffalo
for sport.

Why didn't they see
the balance the harmony
of a people lost in time
time standing still?

What did they achieve
by upsetting nature
tipping the balance
destroying us?

Did they stop war?
Did they stop disease?
Did they stop poverty?
Did they find happiness?

Now their lives are empty
They live with fear
They live with guilt.
What did they gain?

Our spirits still walk the earth.
Their bodies walk the earth.
Their spirits are dead.
What did they win?

Now even they ask why.
Have they finally learned that
when they destroyed us
they destroyed the world?

She Loves Me

I'll be home late tonight
please feed the dogs.
Busy weekend
frozen pizza in the frij.
Women's group Saturday
I'll be late.
What about sex
Sorry I don't need it.
I do love you
just don't need it anymore.
But I'll make you happy
just plan it ahead of time.
around my schedule
I'll satisfy you.
A day for us?
Sorry the grandkids are coming.
should have told me
very busy you know.
really do love you
just don't have time.
Gee, you were great
mind if we watch TV now?

God

Let me see if I've got this straight.
You say he's all powerful,
all loving,
knows all,
the future,
the past.
So he causes good and bad, right?
Oh, I see.
Bad is caused by Satan.
So God knows all,
the future,
the past,
all powerful,
but doesn't cause bad things.
That's Satan.
causes war, disease, hate.
So God is all powerful,
but doesn't cause bad things.
God good.
Satan bad.
God all powerful,
loving
doesn't cause bad things.
Let me see if I've got this straight.

Husband and Wife

We go to work, is it really worthwhile,
when we only end up in a large dirt pile?
Does it really bring real meaning to life,
when all we seem to live with is strife?
Day in, day out, we just keep on,
trying and struggling then someday we're gone.
They bury you and say such wonderful lies.
He was such a good man and always tried.
Such a wonderful husband was he.
Would your widowed wife really agree?
Or inside her heart is she really glad,
to finally be rid of such a cad?
Putting on an act and trying to grieve,
to satisfy the public, but secretly relieved.
Her life goes on, and now she feels alive.
For such a long time she had lived a lie.
And you dear husband if you could do it again,
would you hold me and love me until the end?
Or would it still be the same, all else coming first,
until my heart turned cold, and I put you in the dirt?
Please think about it my dear friend.
How will she remember you when your life ends?

But you dear wife, what about you?
Is it really my fault
you turned into a shrew?
Nagging and bitching
you can't leave it alone.
Is it any wonder I'm happy I'm gone?
I know I wasn't always the best,
and I guess I failed at all your tests.
But I always tried to do what's right.
Loyal and true, home every night.
I finally learned that nothing was enough,
and being dead is not quite so tough
because I'm at peace, and you've got your life.
But with a tongue that cuts like a knife,
who will you love and who will love you?
Do you really think you can start anew?
I was what I was, and you are what you are,
Maybe you'll find someone at a bar.
That's all you deserve is one-night stands,
and I'll be here watching to give you a hand
as your life falls apart and you get what you wrought.
Do these words give you cause for thought?

Reflection

Who is that man standing there in the mirror?
A man growing old, no longer young and fair.
It can't be me, his hair is so white.
When did he turn into such a blight?
When did his chin begin to sag?
Underneath those eyes, do I see a bag?
What are those rolls around his waist?
Of old age is he beginning to taste?
His chest is falling toward the ground,
and his voice has a wheezing sound.
Like an old iron pipe, he's beginning to rust.
It won't be long, and he'll turn to dust.
His manhood looks so shriveled and pale,
and most of the time now, it seems to fail.
What are those brown spots on his skin?
Is this a battle, he'll never win?
Will it mean anything when he's gone,
or was it all a waste while time passed on?
Thank God, it's not me, it's someone else,
that lives in that body that's gone to hell.
I feel so sad for that man in the mirror,
longing for the life he once held so dear.

Smiles

Charlie

For a pretty good boss

Where did Charlie go his office is dark
Did he sneak away for a lark in the park
or to sip a few while the hour is happy
or snuggle with Florence and get a little sappy
Will he be back I guess not this time
Now he can relax and sip on the wine
as he watches Rush and cusses Hillary
while sitting and relaxing under a tree
Yes he's gone what will we do
He'll be replaced by we don't know who
But with Charlie gone it won't be the same
At least we'll have someone new to blame
for the screwups for which Charlie is legend
Only kidding folks now let's give a hand
For a boss who was loyal and kind and true
to his family and us and the company too
who knows how to live and now must go on
to that life after work we hope he has fun
We wish it was us but our day will come
and like Charlie we'll all become bums

Earthquake

A rumble deep in the house
awaking me with a start
windows rattling
the floor trembling
glassware tinkling, falling
I hide under the covers
eardrums pounding
my body trembling
with fear trying to
hold off panic
the dogs frantically barking
the cat hiding under the bed
My wife beside me
still sleeping
how can she sleep
I move closer to her
the sound increases
I cover my ears with my pillow
She rolls over
Suddenly the earthquake is over
faster than it began
Was it really an earthquake
I think perhaps it was only my wife
snoring

Birthday

A special day that comes once a year
an excuse to party and enjoy some cheer
blow out some candles on a special cake
one year closer to attending my wake.
When we're young it's so much fun
to sing and laugh 'til day is done.
Now that I'm older I'd rather skip it
but the wife would have a fit.
So the kids come over and we party some.
At least (I think) we're having fun.
I'd much rather be off the hook
to listen to music or read a book
or to watch TV or take a nap
but I play the game and take the rap
of being wiser and older by a year
while I enjoy some frosty beers.
Plus every year I have to face it
that I'm winding down a little bit.
And that special day just reminds me
that I'm one year closer to eternity.
But if they forgot I know I'd be sad.
So let's party on for the sake of this lad.
And I'll force myself for the sake of others.
Are they having fun or do they also have druthers?

A Stupid Poem

This is just a stupid poem.
I think I'm ready to go home.

I'm tired of working so gosh darn hard.
I think I'll eat a cup of lard.

I'm tired of getting up in the morning.
I have some socks that need some darning.

I'm getting old and tired and fat.
Now where did I leave my baseball hat?

I don't get horny as oft' as before.
I think I'll take a walk to the store.

My electric blanket just conked out.
I think I got a case of the gout.

My alarm clock again forgot to go off.
Maybe I'll play a round of golf.

My house needs painting be sure it's true.
Would you like to share a cup of glue?

My roof is leaking, oh dear me.
I think I have to take a pee.

Where am I, am I really here?
It must be time for another beer.

My fly is open, so I'm told.
It's no wonder I feel so cold.

I just woke up my wife is gone.
How will I ever carry on?

Oh I hear her now I guess she's back.
She was probably feeding the kitty cat.

We have no water, I think it's the pump.
Now I have to take a dump.

I'm almost done, I'm near the end of the page.
Please don't go into a state of rage.

Maybe this poem was a waste of time,
but my only purpose was to rhyme.

Ice Cream

2 or 3 scoops of vanilla (maybe even 4)
chocolate sirup dripping, flowing
over around those white mounds
sounds almost sensuous
not almost it is sensuous
a hot summer night
riding in the back seat of the car
out with mom and dad
licking that ice cream cone
chocolate chip
chocolate ripple
chocolate twirl
cookies and cream
et cetera et cetera et cetera
a cold winter night wind blowing
sitting by the fireplace
eating ice cream
shivering in ecstasy
maybe not as good as making love
a real close second.
Could I have just a little more?
Please?

Sonnets

Time

Time sometimes it seems to fly
or drag on and on throughout the day
until the sun begins to die
and with my love again I lay.
I hold you close and feel your skin
pressing against me and warming my life
shielding me from the world's din
and freeing me from this land of strife
But time keeps moving and soon we sleep
the night coming through while we silently dream
and after awhile dawn begins to creep
and the sky and the earth begin to show a seam
We awake touching and feeling a morning chill
Time continues to come and go at will.

Came a Star

There came a star so long ago
on a cold and wintry night
while we toiled in a world of woe
'til we looked up to that heavenly light.
He descended on the wings of a dove
and his light remains in the midst of dark
bringing the truth of eternal love
to a world so cold and damp and dark.
Sometimes we forget that he's always there
loving and caring for all his creation
while we sink deeper into dispair
and further away from Him we run.
But now and then we try to remember
the star that was born long ago December.

I See Him

I see Him everywhere throughout the day,
in the trees, the sky, the rippling streams,
He'll always be with us, come what may,
even at night in the midst of our dreams.
In the lick of a puppy against my face,
the warmth of your hand held in mine,
in the beauty of clouds like delicate lace,
the gentle tickle of a sparkling wine.
In the velvet touch of your lips on my cheek,
in the cool breeze against the back of my neck,
when I kneel to pray throughout the week,
His keeping my life from being a wreck.
I see Him everywhere in joy and strife.
Thank you, Lord, for giving me life.

Talk to Me

Please tell me everything that you hold dear,
your life, your thoughts, your hopes, your fear.
Sometimes you seem so quiet and afraid.
Open your heart and feel the love we made.
Open your eyes and look into mine.
Drink in my love like inspiring wine.
Please share your laughter and your tears,
crying together, let my heart hear,
the pain and the sorrow that won't let you go.
Let me feel it with you until it is no more.
And if it won't free you, I won't leave you there,
alone and afraid and filled with despair.
I'll always be with you today and forever,
so love me tonight and leave me never.

My Love

My love for you is like the warmth of the sun,
and doesn't cool with the evening dew,
which glistens o'er everything when day is done,
when I thank God that you love me, too.
Tomorrow will be another day,
we'll arise and begin the daily grind,
until again at last we relax and lay
together while our hearts and bodies bind.
In this world, it's very tough
to keep love alive for so many years,
and sometimes we fight and say that's enough,
but that's only the world feeding our fears.
So I'll love you forever my beautiful one,
and we'll be together when day is done.

The Flood of 93

Cool refreshing running down my face
splashing through gutters and miniature lakes
Refreshing the earth and giving it life
the noise and grandeur of a lightning strike
But too much came instead it brought death
drowning the earth 'til nothing is left
but mud and a river that cannot be tamed
while nature plays out its cruel game
towns wash away and people lose hope
trying to survive life's vicious joke
and not far away the nation's in drought
wells drying up tomorrow in doubt
but like long ago the rainbow appears
the covenant renewed for the coming years.

A Shield Against Fear

Whenever I touch you it gives me a start
arousing a fire deep in my heart
beating so fast will it ever stop
until at last I finish my part
that final spasm that seems like a dream
relaxing and holding each other close
is this what life really means
lying together in a lover's pose
and all too soon the night slips away
we slowly awake still touching our skin
and we start to face the coming day
trying to survive the world's din
  waiting for night to bring heaven so near
  when love again shields us from a world of fear.

Stereo Memories

Lives Come and Go

In memory of Margaret Timpner, Bowman Sharp, Lenny Scinto and Jim Christopher.

An eventful year 1994,
some good, some bad, some just okay.
Dad had to pass through that final door,
that I'll have to face on a future day.
I'm still sad and afraid, I'm that kind of guy,
going on with a memory,
and though I keep looking for more time to buy,
someday it will be me you no longer see,
because for us all time soon runs out,
so we must laugh and play and love today,
though still I live with fear and doubt,
trying to keep the end at bay.
But here's to those who finished the fight,
to Margaret and Dad and Lenny and Jim,
and for all the others who brought us light
until they had to leave to be with Him.
None of you were here long enough,
but that's the nature of the life of a friend,
that going too soon always makes it tough
for those still heading toward the final end.
So thanks for being here for part of my life.
It's a better world because of you,
and though your deaths cut me like a knife,
because you were here, the world stayed new.

Lenny

In memory of Lenny Scinto

He died.
Just sitting there at his desk
after lunch.
I was on vacation
when the call came.
I guess I wasn't real surprised.
He was a lot older than me,
health problems,
overweight.
Maybe he was ready.
Maybe it was what he wanted.
His wife already gone.
Living alone.
I'll never know if that's
the way it was.
But I know I wasn't ready
for him to go.
It's always too soon.
Always.

The Shoebox

There it was
under Dad's bed
a plain shoebox with
some old news clippings
a money clip
dance programs
a bunch of those old
license plate keychain tags
some organization used to send out
a poem I'd written as a kid
some old letters
from my college years
tied up with a shoestring
letters from Mom
letters from me to Mom
from Larry (he's dead now)
from a girl named Jo Ann
from two girls named Joan
one I remember
one I don't
but none of Her letters
(I was hoping for at least one)
But I remember
throwing them away
in a dumpster
by the dorm
trying to erase a memory
that won't erase

Lorene

In memory of Lorene Mattson

She never grew up
seventy plus and going strong
dating dancing laughing
still bragging about her tiny waist
not a perfect life
troubled marriages
troubled children
but could always laugh
planning a family reunion
two months
before she died
but time caught up
and she was gone in an instant
In my mind she's still there
fresh and alive and laughing
That's the kind of person
she was

He Was Old (But Not That Old)

In memory of Jim Christopher

He was old, but not that old
but time is something we can't control
His hair was gray, but not that gray
Mine was grayer on that day
But I'm still here, and he is gone
A day in June ended his song
I miss him so what else is new
Lives come and go and the sky is blue
People make love and babies are born
and hope returns on an Easter morn
but still I cry for the life that was
while I continue to search for a cause
for living, for loving, for just going on
when hope is fading like the setting sun
but I know the sun will come again
and clouds and rain and flowers anew
and I hope it isn't all in vain
here for awhile, then gone into the blue
and those I loved will cry as they must
ashes to ashes, dust to dust.

It Wasn't Them

Not my mom and dad
It wasn't them
not really
I've been to nursing homes before
people staring
waiting
Is there anything behind those stares
Mom and Dad can't really be that old
I know if I went home
they would still be there
like always
nothing changed
Did it really happen
It seems like a blur that
flew by
The house is now only a house
wood and brick and shingles
could be anyone's house
I can't go home anymore
All I can do is wait

A Lifetime

In memory of Billy Baird

When Billy died, I was confused. I still am.
Why couldn't we play together awhile longer?
a few more games of catch,
a few more Cub Scout meetings,
a little more mischief?
Why did I get to grow up?
Why did I get to fall in love?
Why didn't he get that chance?
to love a woman,
to feel her wrapped around his body,
around his heart, around his soul?
Why couldn't you let him have that?
to have his own children,
to love them, laugh and cry with them,
to tear his hair out over them,
to play with his grandchildren?
What difference could it have made to you?
Don't you have enough friends already,
that you had to take mine?
I'm told you're a loving god.
Maybe I'm selfish.
What does that make you?
He was only here for a lifetime.
It wasn't enough.

Moms and Dads Should Always Be

Why did they have to grow old
Why can't I face it
the pending death
of Mom and Dad
Or is it my death
that I can't face
the fact that when they're gone
I'm next in line
the repeating cycle
over and over
sperm meets egg
birth
life
ashes
and it starts over
again and again
It's coming
I can't stop it
But why them
Moms and Dads
should always be

That Old Hick Town

While I was growing up
all I could think about was
leaving that old hick town
I went off to college lucky me
got married moved far away
Gee looking back
I kind of miss that old hick town
So I visit once in awhile
look up old friends
thrilled to see me and likewise
but something's missing
Somehow they're different
had to build a life without me
I used to hate that old hick town
Old buildings got torn down
new ones went up
That old hick town I hated is gone
and somehow I just can't love
the one that replaced it.

Yesterdays

Where did they go, those endless years?
Did they die with the laughter
or drown with the tears?
Will the love we knew be the love we know,
and will it get better as the time still flows?
And when time stops, what of then?
Will we still be together over the bend?
What has happened, where did they go?
Why are my memories like melted snow?
Why are the kids so big and tall?
Why is my back against the wall?
When we met, was it only chance,
or since time began were we meant to dance?
I know the latter is what's true.
The first day we met, I knew.
I had some loves, I had some fun.
One day I met the real one.
Is that the way it's meant to be
you and me? (is that reality?)
I don't say much, but you know that I feel.
Never doubt that my love is real.
You might rather have a sweetheart rose,
but sometimes we don't always get what we chose.
But I got you and you got me.
Is that enough for eternity?

I Can Still See Her

In memory of Margaret Timpner

I can still see her in my mind,
so close, so real, but out of time.
She really had a long, full life,
a woman, a mother, a loving wife.

I can still see her in her house,
cooking, cleaning, loving her spouse.
It seems so empty now that she's gone,
but still so full as memories linger on.

I can still see her in your face,
your eyes, your mouth, even God's grace.
She lives in you, although she's missed.
Can't you still feel her kiss?

She can still hold you in her arms,
her warmth against you calming your storms,
Just close your eyes, and she'll be there,
wiping away all of your tears.

Time does not stop, even for us,
ashes to ashes, soon we'll all be dust,
but love goes on, forever and ever.
Does anything else really matter?

Sunrise

In memory of Bowman Sharp

When sun sets on a life, what does it mean?
Somehow it almost seems obscene.
A withered old body is put in the ground.
It seems like we ought to be more profound.
We long for the life that once was so real,
and pray that the grave is not really a jail.
They live in our minds, so slowly to fade.
Is that all that's left, just death and the grave?
We want to have hope, but sometimes it's hard,
when from seeing or loving them, you are barred.
But the next morning the sun comes alive,
warming your face, and you arise
to see the beginning of another day,
and little by little your thoughts drift away.
You start to remember the times that were good,
when you held each other, love starting to bud.
You think back farther to when you first met,
so young, so shy, you'll never forget.
And you smile at the memory, it seems so real,
closing your eyes trying to hold what you feel.
And the tears start to come, flowing so free
remembering the times of just you and he
when you laughed and played and life was so right
but time had to keep on 'til things weren't so bright
So let the tears flow, let them wash away your pain,
and remember tomorrow, the sun will rise again.

It's Been a Long, Long Time

It's been a long, long time, decades in fact.
I wonder if she looks old and fat.
It's been a long, long time, so many years.
I wonder if she has gray hair.
It's been a long, long time, since she had me beguiled.
Did she ever walk down the aisle?
It's been a long, long time, half a century.
Does she ever think of me?
It's been a long, long time, will I see her again?
And we'll talk about remember when.
It's been a long, long time, where is she now?
I wonder if she looks like a sow.
It's been a long, long time, why do I care?
So what if we once had some good times to share.
It's been a long, long time, she's just a memory.
Have her years been good as they were for me?
It's been a long, long time, but still I'm haunted.
The feelings won't leave though they're not wanted.
It's been a long, long time, but now she's gone.
Why is it so hard for me to move on?
It's been a long, long time, God help me put her aside.
Why is she still taking me for a ride?
It's been a long, long time, have I lost my mind?
Why am I possessed by that different time?
It's been a long, long time, another loves me now.
Lord, don't let me lose her too, somehow.

Mischief, Incorporated

In memory of Mike Simmons

Some people you forget
Not Mike
Yes there really are people with
eyes that twinkle
who with a serious look on their face
are really laughing inside
who never grow up
Oh he became a man all right
got married
became a dad
But inside I know what he was
still a kid
One of the lucky ones
No time to let life get him down,
No time to let the world defeat him
Sure we miss him
But he went out a winner
Why so young why so fast
Who knows
It happens
People come and go
Those we love always go too soon
But I can't think of Mike
without a smile on my face

Bowman

It's my middle name.
it was also my dad's middle name.
Dad was a gentleman,
devoted to Mom,
Caring for her in her
failing years when
he was failing himself.
A man I look up to.
It's a proud name (means archer).
One of my childhood heroes was
Robin,
also a bowman,
devoted to his followers
and to Marian.
Dad and Robin are gone now
and Mom.
But I'm proud to
share his name.
Bowman.
Has a nice sound
doesn't it?

Stereo Memories

Why did you leave old friends of mine?
Why did you die before your time?
You brought such joy but now we grieve.
Why did you take such early leave?

Holly sang and went down in flame.
On a New Year's Eve Ricky's family grieved.
The Dorseys can no longer play me a tune,
and Glenn Miller could be the man in the moon.

Some of you lived to a ripe old age.
Some died young and we screamed with rage.
Death is the one we cannot bluff,
but the life of a friend is never long enough.

But my friends still live on the TV shows,
and whenever I wish on the stereo.
We laugh and cry as if they're alive,
and swing and sway to that G.I. jive,

dance and swoon to a Dorsey tune
underneath the light of an autumn moon
while fumbling our way thru a world of pain
and wondering what there is to gain

by making believe that they're still here
and covering up those bitter tears.
Their music will always be in my mind
even though it's out of a different time.

Elvis my friend what can I say?
I hope you've found some better days.
You sang it all the rock and the slow,
but now you just live in my stereo.

Nat the King a love song could sing.
A velvet softness to a song he would bring,
and Judy is over the rainbow now,
her song coming thru still clear and proud.

Bing would sing he was dreaming of,
while we kissed gently and shared our love
by the flickering light of a fire bright,
lost in the hope of a Christmas night.

Roy we're running scared and oh so lonely.
How did you survive such tragedy?
In your songs you could do no wrong,
but your heart gave out and you had to move on.

Bobby is there beyond the sea
somewhere lost in eternity.
Your easy rock plays on forever.
Did you ever find your dream lover?

Dell why did you run away?
We're sorry you felt that you couldn't stay.
It's a world of pain with little to gain.
Perhaps in forever you're out of the rain.

Ricky's gone to live in lonesome town,
turning our world upside down.
We always love to listen to you.
Please send our love to Mary Lou.

Guy we think of you New Years Eve.
The joy of the night makes it hard to grieve.
But we still dance to the sound of your band.
Your music will forever be our friend.

John, it makes me laugh when I try to imagine
if there's such a thing as a beatle heaven.
Are you still writing music in the stars
and crying for us and our stupid wars?

But my stereo can release them all,
and deep in my heart I hear their call
to dance to the tune of a happier life
when it seemed the world lacked such strife.

So many more it's hard to keep track.
The sounds and memories keep coming back.
And I hum those tunes from yesteryear,
still loving old friends I hold so dear

as I lay back to take a nap,
but then my foot begins to tap,
and my mind becomes a concert hall
while I dance again at the Harvest Ball.

So when I'm down and things aren't right,
and I lay awake and brood at night,
I turn on a tune inside my mind,
to take me back to an earlier time

when the world seemed right and love was new,
and passion didn't cool with the morning dew,
and cheek to cheek we twirled around
enchanted by the wonderful sound

in those endless nights of long time past
until finally at last
sleep comes along to put me at rest,
and I snuggle tight inside my nest,

humming a tune inside my dreams,
and for that too brief night it seems
I've travelled back to that former time
when the songs were new and life was fine,

and our feet never tired of dancing all night,
and love was pure and the future was bright,
sharing our passion under a starlit sky,
never dreaming of saying goodbye

to those wonderful friends with talent so real,
sounds I not only heard but also could feel,
but deep in my soul a warmth turning cold
as one by one they left the fold,

never to be seen only to be heard
in those stereo speakers are the words
of a time flown away never to return,
and deep in my heart I feel that burn

of tears welling up out of control,
breaking my heart and taking its toll
as I face the truth that they're really gone,
and only in memory can they linger on,

their bodies cold inside the ground,
their only life a recorded sound,
of stereo memories out of the past
and life goes on until at last,

I'll be with them for eternity,
and I'll sing and dance as they play for me,
sending a warmth up and down my spine,
and I'll drink them a toast with heavenly wine

in gratitude for the joy they give
and a charge to those of you who live,
to never forget that time in the past
when life and love was not so fast.

There was time for talk and play and fun
and time for two to really become one
and kids to grow up just being kids.
Life was real and warm and not on the skids.

So if you really want to feel aglow,
turn off the TV turn on the stereo.
Hold each other close and close your eyes.
Go back to the time when they were still alive,

and dance the night away with not a care.
For a moment in time learn to share
those marvelous tunes that now only live
in metal and tape but still can give

a hope and warmth that can never die
as long as we keep the sound alive,
style and melody, harmony too
sounding so old but forever new,

and feel their love flooding into your heart,
your fingers drumming playing the part
along with those friends who no longer can be
because they're only a memory,

trapped in the stereo only to leave
out of the speakers sound starting to weave,
but it's only memories from the past,
and time continues to fly so fast.

So hold each other tight while you can.
Dance and swing to the sound of the band.
Keep love alive it's all that counts,
and never forget the wonderful sound

of stereo memories no longer real.
Open your heart and let it really feel
their hearts and minds especially the love
that they continue to send from above.

I know that quite often I return to the past,
and sometimes it brings me a joy that lasts
for maybe an hour, maybe a day,
making the present less of a haze

and helping me through some lonely nights
trying to recall when things looked bright
feeling my way through an ache in my heart
even though I'm only playing a part.

So return to the past whenever you can.
Tap your feet to the sound of the band.
It doesn't hurt to remember what was
and it may help you continue a better cause

of bringing back love to a world without hope
so much pain so many can't cope.
We all have to try, I can't do it alone.
It must go on 'til life is done.

Join me now and listen to the tunes.
Return with me to those warm nights of June
when love was warm and we were so alive.
Our bodies were jumping to the sound of the jive.

Let it refresh your soul as you revel in the sound
of love and hope that knew no bounds
Let yourself go don't be afraid.
Let yourself drink of those better days.

And then lay back and close your eyes,
thanking the Lord they were once alive.
Though now they're gone, the music lives
because my stereo knows how to give

the sounds of a time that once was so real,
and all of those friends inside me I feel,
and though I may hide some bitter tears,
I thank God that they once were here.